Video Marketing in 2019 Made (Stupidly) Easy

Vol.2 of the Small Business Marketing Made (Stupidly) Easy Collection

by Michael Clarke

Founder, Punk Rock Marketing

Published in USA by: Punk Rock Marketing

Michael Clarke

ISBN-13: 978-1-970119-11-4

Table of Contents

About the Author

Michael Clarke is a former cubicle monkey turned social media marketing consultant and author.

He is also the owner of the world's most neurotic Jack Russell Terrier.

Also By Michael Clarke

TWITTER MARKETING IN 2019 MADE (STUPIDLY) EASY

FACEBOOK MARKETING IN 2019 MADE STUPIDLY EASY

PINTEREST MARKETING IN 2019 MADE STUPIDLY EASY

INSTAGRAM MARKETING IN 2019 MADE STUPIDLY EASY

LINKEDIN MARKETING IN 2019 MADE STUPIDLY EASY

EMAIL MARKETING IN 2019 MADE STUPIDLY EASY

SEARCH ENGINE OPTIMIZATION IN 2019 MADE STUPIDLY EASY

A Special FREE Gift for You!

If you'd like FREE instant access to my seminar "How to Make a Damn Good Living With Social Media (Even If You Hate Social Media" then head over to **PunkRockMarketing.com/Free**. (What else you gonna do? Watch another "Twilight" movie?!)

Prologue: Why You're a Total F#*$& Moron If You Don't Do Video

I remember the first time I heard the phrase, "THIS is the YEAR you MUST do Video…"

That was 2009. (Pretty sure I made a note in my Blackberry at the time.)

Since then, it seems, every nanosecond some rambling pundit, myself included, comes out with their prediction about how THIS is the year video will dominate everything…

…and how any small business owner who doesn't RIGHT NOW, THIS VERY MINUTE drop everything they're doing and pick up a video camera and create 45 YouTube videos…

…will fall into bankruptcy, lose their livelihood and wander the streets in a disoriented post-marketing stupor.

The truth is: RIGHT NOW represents an absolute, goldmine opportunity for marketers to do video.

Because creating, promoting and distributing your videos has NEVER been easier.

The best part: YOUR customers don't know that.

Most people are impressed by the fact it took you all of THREE MINUTES to talk to an electronic device with a blinking light…

…then spent the extra SEVEN MINUTES to cut out the boring parts where you forgot to turn the camera off…

…and then dedicated a monumental THIRTY SECONDS it took to upload the video and give it a title that isn't totally pointless.

So, before we jump into the nuts-and-bolts of video marketing (and there are quite a few nuts-and-bolts to contend with), here are a few major-league kick-ass reasons video marketing is not only an effective and rather inexpensive way to market to new customers…

…but a totally revolutionary way to do business.

Kick-Ass Reason No. 1: Video Marketing is Cheap

But what about all that gear? And expensive editing software and all the time to memorize aspect ratios and HD video export formats?

Relax. Breathe.

Yes, there MIGHT be an initial investment in some gear. (If ya got a smartphone, that expense can be greatly minimized.)

But when it comes to managing your marketing costs — namely trying to get a ton of leads without taking out a second mortgage —

video is the MOST EFFECTIVE and CHEAPEST FORM of marketing there is.

Just TRY to get on the first page of Google with a keyword-infused article on your website, or even worse, some clumsy Google PPC campaign.

And while your competition waits six months for the Googlebots to index their blog post or pays $7.50/click in an ultra-spendy Adwords campaign, you and I can rip off a quick video and get my video on the first page in a matter of a week. At nearly 10% of the cost. (About as kick-ass as it gets.)

Kick-Ass Reason No. 2: Video Marketing is Fast

And while your competitors spend two hours on that 400-word opus that Google may or may not rank them for…you and I can create ten videos and have an entire video editorial calendar wrapped up for the next two-and-a-half months.

And I say this as a guy who loves writing. (I'm

one of those hopeless English Majors who actually read, and liked, "Moby Dick.")

But writing moves at GLACIAL speed compared to video. And, let's be honest, when was the last time you READ an entire 400-word "anything" online. (That's what I thought.)

Kick-Ass Reason No. 3: Video Gets Shared a Lot

Know what gets shared the most on Facebook? Pictures of friends AND videos, the social engine that drives the Internet.

So, if you're looking to boost business at your burger joint, instead of pouring thousands of dollars into offline print marketing or PPC campaigns that have crappy ROIs…

…just make a funny behind-the-scenes video of your kitchen crew, and you'll get a much bigger bang for your marketing buck.

Kick-Ass Reason No. 4: Video Puts a (Human) Face to Your Business

All that snappy sales copy and reams of direct-mail pieces won't make people feel nearly as connected and interested in you, and your business, as video.

I could tell you it's because 90% of our judgments are based on what we can see. (Though that might be a part.)

I think the real reason is that video, by the medium's nature, just "feels" more intimate and personal. (Especially for the viewer.)

I can't tell you how many emails I've gotten from people who saw one of my vids and felt like they just "knew" me. (Stalker-ish? Yes. Good for business? Absolutely!)

And if you approach your video marketing with a sense of humor, and a willingness to look foolish, there's nothing that can stop you.

Kick-Ass Reason No. 5: Video Marketing Can Help You Own Your Market

I've done it countless times, where I've entered a market with long-time old-school established search-engine competition…

…and BLOWN them away in a matter of a few weeks with three or four strategic videos.

That's because videos give you instant credibility. And help differentiate you as a seriously big fish in a super-sized pond.

Because if most businesses dip their toe into video marketing, they suck at it. And most people are lazy and don't want to read anything more than a paragraph.

But give 'em a couple two-minute videos and they'll be putty in your hands. And, luckily, you can sell a whole lot of crap to putty.

Chapter 1: Which Kind of Video Should You Do?

"If you don't make mistakes, you aren't really trying."
-Coleman Hawkins

So, what'dya need in a perfect piece of video marketing?

Well, not much marketing, for one. (But we'll get to that.)

First, let's break down some different forms of video marketing and see which may or may not be a good fit for your business needs.

Video Form No. 1: Talking-Head Expert Stuff

Just like it sounds.

This is somebody on your team, or maybe you, talking straight to a camera or smartphone mounted on a tripod, offering helpful tips on a topic.

It's simple, powerful and staggeringly effective for building rapport with viewers.

Mostly, because so many videos of this kind are truly abysmal. (Just head over to the freakshow that is YouTube to verify this painful fact.)

As with any video: audio quality is huge. Nobody will tolerate you talking 40 feet away from the camera into an external boom mic.

It can also be scary, especially for people who aren't Uber-comfortable on camera; in which case a script or series of bullet points is highly recommended.

Pros: Personable. Quick. Easy to produce. Great

at building an emotional connection to you or your brand.

Cons: May require Valium for those frightened of being on camera.

Video Form No. 2: Screen-Capture Tutorial

This is where you record what's on your computer screen, whether it be a PowerPoint presentation or a software demo, with software such as Camtasia or Screenflow.

I know. Sounds mind-numbingly boring, but it's great for:

- Product Demos
- Sales Videos
- Technical Training
- Big Ideas That Require Text

And you know that whole "rule" about corporate PowerPoint presentations? Where you're not supposed to repeat the words on the slide?

Yeah, that doesn't apply here.

In a video, people actually like to read along as you go through the points of your presentation.

The downside is you don't get that intimate connection you do with "talking head" videos, but you know what? For some folks that's okay.

If you're camera-shy, this can be a great way to break into the video marketing field. (Without taking that paper bag off your head.)

Pros: Don't even need a camera! Easy to fix glitches and mistakes. Super cheap and easy to make.

Cons: Can be boring, if not focused. Need images to make video stand out.

Video Form No. 3: Behind the Scenes

This is self-explanatory; a video that shows viewers a behind-the-scenes look at your business.

Now, this may require you to tap into your inner Spielberg. But if you can, it can be worth it.

Ya just wanna go around your business and shoot some footage. Talk to your employees, give folks a look at what's it like behind the counter. Show people that your business is filled with…well…people.

Even if you're a solo-preneur, people still want to see what your desk looks like, what books are on your bookshelf, what kind of Star Wars bobbleheads you have in the window, etc. (I'm a "Boba Fett" guy, but maybe that's just me.)

We'll cover filming later, but here's the absolute KEY to a good behind-the-scenes vid: get good audio.

Too many of these behind-the-scenes videos have such bad audio, it makes them unwatchable. And don't talk about how amazing your company is. Talk about something interesting.

Got a policy where employees can bring their dogs to work? Film it!

Have somebody on your team who can break dance? Film it!

Is there an annual chili contest in the second-floor building of your company? Film it!

This is a great way to spotlight your team and get some cool marketing exposure in the process.

Pros: Really good (sneaky) way of marketing your brand. Fun. Boosts team morale.

Cons: Requires some editing time. Bit of technical know-how. (But not much.)

Video Form No. 4: Customer Testimonials

This is actually the most overlooked form of video marketing, but one of the most powerful.

Got a group of regular customers who love your stuff? Film them! Just have them do a brief 30-second talk about why they love your stuff.

(**Tip:** Be sure they start their response with "The reason I love (name)…" or else it will be hard to edit their response in context.)

Sell things virtually?

No problem. You can record people on Skype talking about your company, or even better…

Have them leave a voice mail message and put that into a video with a simple slideshow. (God knows why, but people just instantly believe things that are recorded on the phone.)

Now, you want to tread carefully here. Don't make it too over-the-top. (No need to have scores of customers gush about how your company is the most amazing thing that ever existed.)

But if you've got some good social proof going on, throw in some video footage of your products or services. It can do more for your video marketing efforts than all the talking-head videos in the world.

Pros: Very effective at increasing leads. Easy to film. Virtually no work on your part.

Cons: Can get very annoying quickly, if not done well. Sometimes hard to get customers to talk on-camera.

Video Form No. 5: Video Q&A

Have no idea what to do a video on?

Well, just ask people what their biggest questions/frustrations are…and then go ahead and answer them.

I had a client of mine who ran a pizza joint, and all he did was set up his iPhone and answer questions submitted to him via email. Think his tips on helping folks create the perfect crust hurt sales?

Absolutely not!

And in a later chapter I'll show you how to track the effectiveness of your video marketing to make sure you're not wasting your time with these types of videos.

Video Form No. 6: Anything But…

Notice what kind of video marketing I did NOT mention?

That's right. YOU talking about how amazing/wonderful/awesome your company is.

Nobody cares. (Really.)

You can talk about virtually anything on

camera, just don't go on and on about the amazing features and benefits of your latest doo-hickey.

Unless it's a sales page video, and even then...

Not only will the "one ring to rule them all" in video distribution, YouTube, probably ban your video, but it won't help you reach any of your marketing goals.

Chapter One Key Takeaways:

- Talking-head videos are great for how-to tips and building personality into your brand.
- Screen-capture videos are fantastic for technical training and product demos.
- Behind-the-scenes vids are perfect for showing a funnier/lighter side of your biz. (Even if you don't have a lighter side.)
- Testimonials from your customers are great if done subtly.
- Video Q&As are a good way to help people out and allow you to be seen as a ready-made expert.
- Overt marketing videos are boring and lame; and nobody wants to watch them.

Chapter 2:
Anatomy of the Perfect Video

"To express yourself needs a reason, but expressing yourself is a reason."

-Ai Weiwei

Okay, so you got some ideas for what kind of video you might want to do. But what do you actually put in the video?

How do you structure your video? What do you say? What do you NOT say?

And how do you make sure the video actually does something for your business, you know, besides pad your ego?

Worry not! Here's my patented (I wish) FIVE

Step Video Marketing Checklist to ensure your videos stay on track and get you the results you want:

Step No. 1: The Brief Intro

When I say brief? I mean…brief. Get in, get out.

And tell people WHY the hell they should be watching.

This is probably the simplest step in this process, but the one most people neglect. (Watch any DIY how-to videos on YouTube and this will become abundantly clear.)

This is what I say in my intro, to establish WHY people should watch, and I hardly ever deviate from this formula:

"Hi there, it's Michael from Punk Rock Marketing. And in this short video, I will cover the No.1 reason Facebook is a spawn of Satan on bringing down Western Civilization with its desire to plant electrodes in our brain…and what you can do about it."

Okay, so let's break it down a bit further:

- **"Hi, it's Michael…"**
- Put your name and your company in there fast. You have no idea where people will watch your video, so get your branding out there right away.
- **"In this short video…"**
- Tell 'em it will be short. This is key. Lets them know they won't be sitting in their chair for a hundred years as you show them how to change a spark plug.
- **"I'm going to cover…"**
- Tell them what they will get from watching the video. What solution will your video provide? What insight will it cover? What PROBLEM will it solve?

Step No. 2: The State of Things

This is where you take a slight step back. And tell people WHY it's important they know this thing you're going to tell them.

They may already intuitively know this, but this brief section will help nail it home, and give them confidence in your ability to help them.

Again, keep this brief.

I might do something like this:

"Facebook has built its empire on user data. But how do they get that data? With tiny electrodes they plant in our brain when we're sleeping next to our smartphone. That's how!

"Here's how you can keep the electrodes from invading your body…"

Notice how it moves seamlessly into the next step which is…

Step No. 3: The Meat and Potatoes

This is where you instruct. Or with more whimsical fare, such as the behind-the-scenes video and testimonials, fire off into the fun part.

Whatever form you're dabbling with, this is

where you give up the goods. Where you deliver on the promise you set forth in the brief intro.

Here are a few tips to ensure your Meat and Potatoes don't go completely off the rails:

- **Don't ramble.** Just stick to the points.
- **Lists are great.** If you can tell us the three steps, five techniques, four tactics to solve the problem…. people will love you for it.
- **Keep the number of steps reasonable.** Don't do 19 ways to lower your car insurance bills. Do seven. Or one.
- **Cover one idea in your video.** You're not trying to cure cancer. You're trying to solve one problem. (Even if that solution has three or four parts to it.)
- **Remember people don't know as much as you do.** If there's a lot of technical jargon or complex ideas, try to keep things simple.

- **Tell stories.** People love personal anecdotes. (As long as they relate to the point. If not, cut 'em.)
- **Don't be boring.**

Step No. 4: The Action Steps

This is where you lay out the simple step-by-step blueprint you outlined in Step No.3 into easily digestible chunks of info anybody can understand.

In my Facebook example:

"First, you cover your head in tin foil. Step two, you bury your iPhone thirty feet below ground…."

If you're doing a talking-head video, and have editing savvy, then you could throw up a quick text image of the steps at the end of the video.

But the key thing is: give people something they can act on right now. (Even though most of them won't.)

Step No. 5: The Call to Action

Okay, you've been a supercool awesome person. You've given them some info and helped improve their lives. (Sorta.)

Now, it's time for them to pay it forward. And, trust me, they will.

Obligation is hard-wired in our brain, so if somebody does us a solid we feel (strongly) the need to pay it back.

So, here's what you do…in the call to action I usually ask people to do two things:

1. Share or comment on my video
2. Grab a free offer/coupon I'm offering

Here's an example:

"If you've enjoyed my anarchist ramblings about the cabal that is Facebook be sure to Facebook like, tweet, or comment in the field below.

"And if you'd like a FREE copy of my new eBook, "7 Ways Facebook is Trying to Eat Your Soul From the Inside

Out," head on over to punkrockmarketing.com to get instant access."

The cool thing about this verbiage is that even if they don't take advantage of your offer, they can still help you out by making your video more popular.

But if they take advantage of the offer, after having watched you talk for 2.5 minutes, they are very much a qualified lead.

Chapter Two Key Takeaways:

- Start your video with a brief intro that tells people what they can expect to find out by watching.
- Follow that up with a short description of why your video is important.
- Get into the meat of your video. Don't ramble!
- Give viewers action steps they can use. Instantly!
- End your video with a call to action that asks people to social share and head over to your website to pre-qualify themselves.

Chapter 3: Getting Geared Up on the Ultra-Cheap

"You can fool all the people all the time…if the advertising is right and the budget is big enough."

-Joseph E. Levine

Video equipment is like computers or guitars.

You can get as complicated and expensive, or as simple and bare-bones as you like. (Much of it will depend on your own personality.)

I'm weird. I LIKE to edit video. (Maybe it's the OCD control-freak in me.)

So, a good copy of video-editing software is a

must for me, but knowing which F-stop setting or white balance control to alter on a camera literally puts me in a coma.

So, with camera choice I want something that looks great out of the box…not something I have to fuss with for hours.

That said, here are my recommendations for the gear you'll need (and may want someday) as you delve into the fabulous world of video marketing.

Remember there are only THREE MUSTS for video: good audio, something to record on, and something to say.

Everything else is just decoration.

Note: *I've created a PDF downloadable Video Marketing Gear Checklist you can use as reference. Be sure to grab your totally FREE copy at: PunkRockMarketing.com/VideoGear*

Video Gear Must-Have No. 1: The Microphone

What??? What about the camera?

I'm telling you, audio is your most important piece of gear.

The quality difference between the cheapest HD camcorder and the most expensive digital SLR is NOTHING compared to the quality difference between internal (built-in) microphones and external sound-capturing devices.

Believe me, the money you spend here will be well worth your while.

Ultra Cheap Option-Lavalier Microphone ($25-$100)

This is a simple tie-clip microphone that attaches to your lapel and plugs in directly into the camera.

Tip: Run the lapel wire under your shirt to avoid making the video look super ghetto.

I used to find these at Radio Shack for about $25. (But then Radio Shack decided to institute "losing money" as a business practice.)

There are a ton of great options on Amazon, including the Sony ECM series. (If you're going to do a bunch of talking-head vids, go for a condenser lav mic. It's worth it.)

Amazon Lav Mics:

PunkRockMarketing.com/LavMic

Elite Option-Wireless Lavalier Microphone ($500-$700)

Okay, I don't expect you to get one of these right out of the gate. But if you make some extra moolah from your video marketing efforts, then adding a wireless lavalier microphone to your video toolbox will be well worth it.

The sound is quite good, considering you're on a wireless channel, and it gives you a ton of flexibility in terms of movement and location. (You can even record live presentations you give.)

Tip: Don't go for the ultra-cheap wireless units. They ain't worth it.

Amazon Wireless Lav Mics:

PunkRockMarketing.com/WirelessMic

Extra Item - iPhone Lav Mic Adapter ($25)

If you plan on shooting exclusively with your smartphone or tablet computer, then you'll need an iPhone adapterhttp://punkrockmarketing.com/iphoneadapter to plug in your lav mic.

Bonus: You can actually get a splitter to let you conduct interviews and get great audio from both you and your subject.

Amazon iPhone Mic Adapter:

PunkRockMarketing.com/iPhoneAdapter

Video Gear Must-Have No. 2: The Camera

Okay. We're here. We're finally gonna get you a camera. (But wait! You might already have one lurking in your shirt pocket.)

Here's a breakdown of some options you have on the camera recording side:

Ultra-Cheap Option - Your Smartphone (Free-$500)

My uncle ran a videography business in the late 80s. His equipment cost him $30,000. Today he could do everything for under $50.

That's because the smartphone you hold in your hand, and will hold for years to come, can produce some amazing QUALITY video.

Now, if you don't have a smartphone, don't run out and go buy one for the video capabilities. It ain't THAT good.

But if you have an Android phone or an iPhone, you've got all you need to produce amazing video. (As long as you know what you're doing; we'll go over that in more detail later.)

Semi-Cheap Option- Rugged Adventure Cameras $95-$200

If you plan on doing a lot of action video — maybe, you run a ski lodge and want to film on the slopes, or you're a surf instructor who wants to shoot some action footage in the water — then there are plenty of rather cheap camera options, such as the GoPro and the Sony ActionCam, that will produce amazing video quality in a variety of rough settings.

The cool thing about these cameras is they're tough and can shoot video (almost) anywhere. Trouble is their sound quality often sucks. (Though they are improving with each new version.)

Mix up your action shots with some microphone

assisted talking segments to get some very usable quality stuff. (No matter where you find yourself.)

Amazon Adventure Cameras:

PunkRockMarketing.com/AdventureCam

Somewhat Elite Option - Prosumer Camera ($400-$800)

The more you spend, the more features you can get with your video camera. Like better lenses, more controls, more stabilization, better ergonomics.

You wouldn't think ergonomics would make a difference. Wait till you have to hold a camera for ten minutes without shaking, you'll see what a difference it makes.

Unfortunately to get the best features around you need to spend upwards of $2500. (At least.)

Unless you go with a "prosumer" camera. These are camcorders that are in the middle region between smartphones and high-end DSLR camera. (And they'll usually set you back, at the high end, just under $1000.)

If you spend money on a "prosumer" model, I recommend you go with a Sony or Canon camera.

There are tons of nice camcorders out there, but these two manufacturers have the best lenses…which are probably the most expensive, and most important, part of a camera.

Amazon Resources: (Sony)

PunkRockMarketing.com/SonyCam

(Canon) PunkRockMarketing.com/CanonCam

UPDATE As I update this section of the book for 2019, I've had a tough time finding a wide selection for this type of camcorder. Canon still makes some good models in this category, but Sony seems to have de-emphasized offering here much.

It's as if they think this smartphone thing is gonna stick around. Word to the wise, buying a Prosumer camcorder now may sound good, but it could be difficult to get parts and service later.

Elite Option - DSLR Camera ($1500-Who Knows?)

This is where I must feign a bit of ignorance - I am not huge camera gear head. (If I were, I'd probably own a $4000 DSLR high-end camera that would make my footage look more amazing than an indie Hollywood film.)

But if you have the budget - and the patience - to work with a high-end camera (lots and lots of accessories are needed) then a high-end DSLR camera will give you the best footage on the planet. (And make your business look so much more profitable and professional than it is.)

Amazon DSLR Cameras:

PunkRockMarketing.com/DSLR

Video Gear Must-Have No. 3: Tripod

Unless you want your videos to induce vertigo, you're going to need a tripod. Here are a few options:

Smartphone Tripods - ($5-$50)

These can range from the arm tripods, ones in which you wrap them around nearly any surface, or traditional stand-on-the-floor models. (Popular brands include Gorilla and Joby, but whatever floats your boat should work.)

Amazon Smartphone Leg Tripod:

PunkRockMarketing.com/PhoneLegTripod

Amazon Smartphone Arm Tripod:

PunkRockMarketing.com/GorillaPod

Camcorder Tripod - ($19-$50)

This will depend mostly on your filming needs. If you're just going to shoot inside, go with one of the cheap, light tripods. (Nothing more than $25.)

If you're going to shoot outside a lot, particularly in windy conditions, you might need something a little more durable, but heavy. (You might even need a few sandbags to hold down the camera. Believe me, wind can be a cruel obstacle to filming.)

Either way, I find tripods generally have the

shelf life of a reality show. (About eight months.)

Amazon Camcorder Tripods:

PunkRockMarketing.com/Tripod

Video Gear Must-Have No.4: Lighting

Now, the lighting you'll need will depend on where you will do most of your filming. If you shoot a lot outside, just use the sun. (It's the best lighting source there is.)

But if you shoot indoors, you're going to need something more than that horrible office neon lighting that makes everybody look like a zombie. So, here are a couple of options:

Super Cheap Option - Home Depot Clip-On Lights ($40)

If you plan to shoot stuff close, like sitting at your desk, or you're just not worried about executing high-quality footage, then a couple of clip-on lights from Home Depot will serve you just fine.

These stark lights can lead to extra shadows, but if you play with the positioning a bit, you can find a nice lighting set up on the ultra-cheap.

Somewhat Cheap Option - Simple Lighting Kit ($100)

I like the lighting kits from FancierStudio. But no matter which brand you use you'll want at least 2 lights - placed behind the camera - that point toward the subject at 45-degree angles.

Now I'm no lighting expert, far from it, but the key is to go for balance. (No intense shadows on the face.) Even crappy lighting can be fixed by boosting the saturation in a video editing program. As long the lighting balanced. But if it's all over the place, then it can be an absolute pain to fix.

Amazon Fancier Studio Lighting Kits:

PunkRockMarketing.com/StudioLighting

Somewhat Cheap Green Screen Option - Green Screen Lighting Kit ($150)

If you plan to do green screen videos - where you'll "key out" the background in your videos and insert a background of your choosing - then buy yourself a lighting kit + green screen combo.

You may need additional lights, but these can be exceptionally versatile. (And can turn even the most cramped office setting into a full-on video studio.)

Amazon Green Screen + Lighting Kit Combo:

PunkRockMarketing.com/GreenScreenKit

Chapter Three Key Takeaways:

- Audio is super important. Invest in a lavalier microphone of some kind to improve your video quality.
- Your smartphone is a fantastic HD camera. (As long as you've got external audio.)
- Tripods are flimsy but required. (You may even need a sandbag or two.)
- Buy cheap desk lamps for a quick infusion of light into your video settings.
- Don't forget to grab your "No B.S. Video Marketing Gear Checklist!"

Chapter 4:
Your Super-Quick 5-Minute

"If you can't explain it to a six-year-old, you don't understand it yourself."

-Albert Einstein

Ya don't have to be Fellini to make great video marketing content. But there are a few, simple rules to making any type of filmed media…

And knowing these rules can make you look way more talented and professional than you are.

So, here's my super-brief Five-Minute Film School Tutorial that you can use to ensure your videos are watchable, compelling and they communicate your message in the best way possible.

Five-Minute Film-School Tip No. 1: Keep the Camera Still

I know there's a zoom button on your camera. That doesn't mean you have to use it.

The problem with the zoom function on most camcorders, and especially smartphones, is that they make the lens more sensitive to things like light, contrast…and your constant frickin' moving.

And, believe me, you're moving even if you're just holding the camera still.

So, put your video device on a tripod whenever you can. And if you need to go "handheld," use a nearby wall or chair to brace yourself.

And if you must "move in" to shoot something close, physically move the camera in. (Not the zoom.) It will look much better in the long run.

Five-Minute Film-School Tip No. 2: Keep the Light Behind You

Most photographers know this trick well, but if you're new to any kind of camera operation, it's a good rule to keep the sun, or major light source, behind you as you film.

The reason is instantly clear to anybody who has filmed on a sunny day. (It makes the subject's face dark and under-exposed.)

Also, if you're filming outside, it's good to know that early morning and late afternoon are the best times to film. (That's because you can control where the sun is.)

Noontime is the absolute worst. (Mid-day sun makes everybody look like zombies. And nobody likes to look like a zombie.)

As for that indoor lighting kit you've got, put your two most powerful light behind the camera at 45-degree angles.

(Here's a quick diagram

[PunkRockMarketing.com/LightingDiagram] you can use for reference.)

And then if you've got another, softer light put that behind the subject to light their back. This will ensure you have decent, balanced lighting.

Five-Minute Film-School Tip No. 3: Keep the Central Subject Out of the Middle

This one surprises some people. I mean, aren't you supposed to put the camera subject in the middle of the frame?

No. It looks sorta weird…and way too geometric.

Instead, put the subject off to the side, with an interesting background filling in the rest of the shot. This will make the video look dynamic and interesting. (Even if the person talking isn't.)

Film-School Tip No. 4: Don't Leave Too Much Headroom

Headroom is that space between a person's head and the top of the frame. It's okay to have a bit, you don't want to cut someone's head off at the forehead.

But you don't want to have too much room at the top. There's an old photography trick, called the Rule of Thirds, which works great here.

Divide the frame into three equidistant horizontal lines (like the flag of Germany) and just make sure the person's head is somewhere near the top half of the frame.

Film-School Tip No. 5: On-Camera Etiquette

For being on-camera, here are a few guidelines to maximize your appearance and overall effectiveness:

- Don't wear sunglasses. People want to see your eyes.
- Wear mid-range colors. (Blues, greens, blacks.) No stripes and no white. (Takes attention away from the eyes.)
- No hats. (Distracts from the face.)
- Don't read from a script. Your eyes will look shifty, and unless you are Tom Brokaw it will be tough to pull off.
- Take a breath, exhale…and then perform. (Don't start without taking a breath…otherwise you'll do a gulp of air in the middle of your performance.)
- Pick one side of the camera to look at and stick with it. (Don't bounce…it will make you look shifty.)

Film-School Tip No. 6: Focus on Helping (Not Your Performance)

If you try to "perform" on camera, if you think

you must somehow embrace your inner news anchor to do well on video, you will be sadly mistaken. The camera has an amazing ability to capture who you are. (Even if you don't want it to.)

And if your entire mindset is all about:

"Look at me! I'm on camera. I'm an expert! Buy my stuff! While supplies last!"

It won't work. (Or not as well as it could.) But if you step into frame and say…

"There's a problem many people have. Here's how I figured out how to solve it. Hope it works for you. Talk to you soon…"

You. Will. Crush. It.

Because so much of the crap videos out there are people yelling at the camera, hoping those "thousands" of viewers will take action NOW!

But if you, or your team, get on camera, and just help solve people's problems, there's no way the competition can stop you.

Chapter 4 Key Takeaways:

- Keep the camera still. Seriously.
- Always keep the sun to your back. (Morning and afternoon are good times to shoot.)
- Put the subject off to the side to mix things up.
- Keep the subject's head in the top third of the frame.
- Don't wear sunglasses, white shirts or hats. Stick to mid-range colors like blue or green.
- Focus on solving people's problems to get past on-camera nervousness.

Chapter 5: Crashing the YouTube Party

"Hobbies of any kind are boring, except for people who have the same hobby."

-Dave Barry

When it comes to looking for a place to house your video marketing efforts, there really is YouTube…and everybody else.

YouTube isn't just simply the largest video-sharing site in the world. It is the second-largest search engine in the world.

Read that again. The second-largest SEARCH ENGINE.

That means, for Internet traffic, there's Google,

then YouTube, then Amazon, then Facebook…

…and then way, way, way down the list are other video-sharing sites such as Vimeo and Viddler and Voohoo (or whatever t they're called.)

This doesn't mean things won't ever change, or that you shouldn't place your videos on other sites. (In a later chapter, I'll show you a super-easy quick way to do so.)

It's just that, when I outline my video-marketing strategy for a project, I spend 99.7% of my time worrying about YouTube. (And then, in between episodes of "Law and Order," I think about other sites.)

YouTube has the eyeballs. (And by last count, nearly 1 billion unique visitors a month.) So that's where your videos need to go.

So, here is my SIX STEP process to uploading your video to YouTube that will increase your exposure and help you add a bunch of new leads into your marketing funnel of doom:

Step No.1: Get a Buddy

Before you upload a single megabyte of video to the YouTube universe, I'd like you to strongly consider adding a powerful mentor/ally/kick-ass video Jedi to your marketing toolbox.

And that is the FREE (though there are paid options) tool: Tube Buddy.

Now before you freak out and say, "I need another marketing tool in my life like I need a six-inch hole in my head," let me give a couple kick-ass reasons this YouTube analysis tool is so awesome.

With a quick install of this Chrome extension — did I mention it's FREE? — you can head over to a popular video in your subject of expertise, or whatever your video is about, and with a click of a button you can:

- Find the best keywords (high traffic; low competition) for your video title
- Find the best tags (high traffic; low competition)

- Nail down the perfect TIME to publish your videos (based on user behavior)
- Collect a list of tags that you can save and manage for future projects
- Track your video ideas (so you don't forget them)

Seriously this tool has not only hours at a time, but exponentially improved my lead-generation efforts on YouTube.

My only complaint is that I could have used this tool about six years ago. (Or maybe I just need a time machine.)

And, yes, you could figure all this stuff out manually. But why put yourself through that?

Try this app out. Your world domination depends on it.

Step No.2: Write a Video Title for Robots and Humans

Writing the perfect video title is equal-parts art

and science. You want a title that contains the RIGHT keywords to get discovered, but you also want to encourage people to consume that video.

And boring, keyword-stuffed titles just won't cut it.

So, what do you do?

I like to incorporate one major keyword in my titles and emphasize how simple and approachable my video is.

I don't want people scared off thinking: "Oh God, that video looks like it's gonna be work." I want them to think: "That video looks short and easily digestible."

That's why I like to use descriptors like:

- "How to"
- "101"
- "Dos and Don'ts"
- "Tips"
- "Tricks"
- "Secrets"
- "Made Easy/Simple"

Let's say I run a blog that caters to would-be romance novelists. (Not sure what I would say to them, but let's go with it.)

And I've done my research in Tube Buddy — my video marketing Obi-Wan Kenobi — and I've found the phrase "Romance Novel Writing" is a good one to use in my title. (It has a score of 87/100 meaning high traffic, low competition.)

Well, I could title my video something like:

- How to Master Romance Novel Writing
- Romance Novel Writing 101
- Romance Novel Writing Dos and Don'ts
- Romance Novel Writing Tips the Competition Doesn't Want You to Know
- Romance Novel Writing Tricks the Pros Use
- Romance Novel Writing Secrets the Bestselling Authors Know
- Romance Novel Writing Made

Easy/Simple/Understandable

You get the picture.

Now in earlier editions of this book, I USED to recommend people put TWO keywords in a title.

Such as:

"Romance Novel Writing Tips 101 | Romance Novel Writing Secrets"

But I have since moved away from that strategy. Not because it doesn't work from a keyword standpoint. It does.

But that over-optimized approach can turn people off. Make the video look overwhelming.

And as any copywriter will tell you, the most powerful weapon you have when writing sales copy is white space.

You want there to be space in your title and description.

As the old saying goes: "The confused mind says 'No.'" And having too much crap in your titles can sometimes lead to more "no's" than you envisioned.

Step No.3: Rename Your Video File According to Your Keyword

This one's a trick few people know about. But the name of your video file directly relates to its ranking and relevancy in YouTube. (And its ranking in good old Google.)

And what do you name it?

The keyword you want to rank for.

So, using the example above, you'd name your file "Romance_Novel_Writing_101" NOT "Video_1."

Now this is something you change on your computer before you upload it to YouTube. But it's super easy. Just click on the folder until the folder name is highlighted, type in the keyword…and you're done. (Simple, but it can really help.)

Step No. 4: Make Sure Your YouTube Channel Is Niche-Focused

If you haven't already created a YouTube account, then this won't be a problem. You'll be starting off with a clean slate and have plenty of room to keep your YouTube channel focused.

But if you've got a channel, and it's got videos of your kids playing soccer, you singing karaoke and that awesome slideshow of your trip to Yosemite…

…then I highly recommend you create a new, separate YouTube channel (you'll need a separate Gmail account as well) that just focuses on your video marketing.

I know it seems like a pain, but it's also part of Google's ranking of the relevancy of videos.

And if all your videos are about "lawn care," then it will assume your channel is about "lawn care." If your video library is a hodge-podge, then you won't get that same benefit of the doubt.

And if you're not sure what to name your

YouTube channel, just pick one of the keywords off the research you just did in Tube Buddy. (Instead of Joe's Pizza Joint…you could do Best Denver Pizza and take advantage of the extra Google juice.)

Step No. 5: Write a Killer Description for Your Video

So, here's where most people screw up. They either have crappy descriptions or no description at all.

Which is sad because the description of your YouTube video is primo real estate. (And super important to how your video will rank in the good old search engines.)

So, your description needs to have five parts and it must be in this order:

1. **A hyperlink to your website.** This must be first and must include the http://…. etc… Example: http://punkrockmarketing.com

2. **Reiterate the FREE/awesome offer you made in the video.** "Head over to punkrockmarketing.com for your FREE copy of my Facebook Brain Protector eBook."
3. **Describe your video.** You are given 1,000 characters here. Use as much of that as you can. And be sure to include that handy-dandy keyword you found earlier a few times in there. If you're not sure what to write about, simply talk about WHY you feel the topic of the video is so important. And then give brief summaries of the steps/topics you cover in the video. (Don't worry, it won't hurt engagement. It will help…a lot!)
4. **Give out your digits.** If ya got a Facebook page, Twitter account, Pinterest doo-dad…whatever…put it here. (Remember to include the http://

part.)

5. **Repeat the FREE offer + your hyperlink.** Example: "Don't forget to head over to http://punkrockmarketing.com for your FREE copy of my Facebook brain protector eBook."

Step No. 5: Beg, Borrow and Steal Your Tags From Your Competitors

This is where Tube Buddy really comes in handy. All you do is:

- Click on the #1-ranked YouTube video for the phrase you want to rank for. (Here, "Romance novel writing.")
- Fire up Tube Buddy and let it analyze the video and find the tags the video creator used to define this video.
- Repeat for the next 2-3 top-ranked videos for that same term.

- Copy all relevant keywords — some might be too obscure to be helpful — and type them into YouTube as your tags.
- Rejoice because you have reverse-engineered your competitor's YouTube success.

Now you don't have to use TubeBuddy to find these tags. You CAN do it manually, by finding a top-ranked video, right-clicking and choosing "View Page Source," and manually finding the keyword embedded in a sea of gibberish-looking code.

And if you're a masochist and enjoy looking at lines of code, then knock yourself out.

But if you want a shortcut to the front of the line, then let Tube Buddy do the tag heavy-lifting for you.

Step No. 6: Upload Your Video

Here's the easy part.

You just click on "upload" at the top of the YouTube navigation and upload your video file, enter your title, description and tags…and you have a published video on YouTube.

But how is anybody gonna FIND your video? Well, that topic of YouTube world domination is what we'll cover in the next chapter.

Chapter Five Key Takeaways:

- Choose a video title that gets a decent amount of traffic and is not competitive. (I use the FREE tool Tube Buddy to figure this out.)
- Re-title the file name of your video using your desired keyword.
- Keep your YouTube channel focused only on video marketing — no personal vids.
- Include a "http://" hyperlink in the beginning of your description.
- Use all 1000 characters of the description if you can.
- "Borrow" tags from other high-performing videos using the Tube Buddy in your corner.

Chapter 6:
How to Promote the Hell Out of Your Video

"I am always doing that which I cannot do, in order that I may learn how to do it."

-Pablo Picasso

If you've gone to the trouble of making a series of videos, then you damn well want to get them in front of the largest number of eyeballs possible.

But most people throw up a video or two on YouTube and simply "wait" for the masses to come banging down their door to give them money.

Sorry, don't work that way.

YouTube requires hustle and some promotional savvy to work. But the cool thing is, once you've got a system (which I'll share with you here) and work that system consistently, it becomes easy to out-pace the competition in no time.

There are basically two different ways to promote your videos:

1. Stuff you can do INSIDE YouTube.
2. Stuff you can do OUTSIDE YouTube.

Let's start with the OUTSIDE stuff. It's super easy and doesn't require much brain power. Here are my THREE YouTube Outside Marketing Strategies I use again and again:

Outside YouTube Promo Strategy No. 1: Promote the Video Everywhere!

Once you upload your video and it's done "cooking" in the YouTube kitchen, you will get a unique URL. (Example: http://youtube.com/watch=S1uDnIP9L)

With that web address in tow, you can now promote that video on social networks like Facebook, LinkedIn, Twitter, Pinterest, Tumblr, your email newsletter, etc.

The key thing is to ASK people to "like" it or "share" it when they watch the video.

Lots of social activity around your video, especially when it's first uploaded, is a big sign to Google that this video is "important" and should be given a prominent place in the search engines. (Both in Google and YouTube.)

Outside YouTube Promo Strategy No. 2: Build Some Links to Your Video

Okay, this technique is a bit on the shady side. (And by shady, I mean if you tried doing this with your own website, Google would send your site to search-engine Siberia.)

But it frickin' works. What you're going to do is build backlinks to the video page.

In the crazy, strange world of SEO (Search Engine Optimization), most people spend time and money trying to get their own websites ranked super quick. (Which doesn't work very often.)

But for a big "authority" site, like YouTube, it can work exceedingly well.

So, here's what you do:

- Head over to Fiverr.com (This is a site where people offer services for five dollars.)
- Search for "SEO" services. (I like to buy ONE "link pyramid," ONE "social bookmarking" gig, and ONE ". Edu Backlink" gig
- Buy THREE "gigs." Choose people with high ratings.
- Have the gig master build backlinks to your video around your primary keyword. (And wait for the traffic to

flow in.)

This won't provide an immediate, overnight boost. But it will help tremendously. (Because hardly anybody else does this.)

Outside YouTube Promo Strategy No. 3: Stop the Presses

If you have a little extra money to spend (about $25) and you've optimized your video to this point, then it's worth your while to send out a press release touting your video.

Huh?

A press release? About a YouTube video?

Before you freak out and tell me that your video isn't newsworthy, and nobody would read a press release about it…

First off, you should see some crap people send press releases on. (It's hysterical.)

Secondly, we are not sending it out in the hope that NBC News is going to ask us to join the broadcast.

We are doing it for the Google backlink love. And Google REALLY respects press releases. (God knows why, most of them are awful.)

For $25 you can head over to a site like WebWire and shoot out a press release about your video.

Couple of keys:

- **Write a decent headline by focusing on the problem you're solving.** Example: "Chicago Pizza King Reveals the Secret to Homemade Crust."
- **Write it in third person.** As if you were having an interview with yourself.
- **Make sure you include links back to the video**, along with the keywords we researched earlier.

Do these three things and you will be light-years ahead of the rest of the schmucks who put their crap on YouTube.

And if you REALLY hate writing, head over to Fiverr and have somebody else write the press release for ya. (Win-win!)

"Forget it, Jake. It's Chinatown."

Okay, now let's jump into the strange morass of insanity and awesomeness that is promotion inside the YouTube universe.

The three main goals of your videos on planet YouTube are:

- Likes
- Shares
- Subscribers

The higher these numbers, the more the Google/YouTube empire will see your video as an authority and you will blow your (feeble) competition out of the water.

So, how do we get more of all that YouTube community goodness? Here are my FOUR favorite strategies for getting more people into your

YouTube army:

Inside YouTube Promo Strategy No. 1: Create YouTube Cards

YouTube cards are a way to create linkable text overlays onto your video. (But they're far better than those old, annoying YouTube annotations that looked as fresh and modern as a dot-matrix printer.)

You can use them to:

- Encourage people to subscribe to your YouTube channel.
- Provide links to your other videos.
- Link over to other YouTube users' videos who offer more resources.
- Have people donate to your cause or kick-starter campaign.
- Most importantly: Provide links over to your WEBSITE!

YouTube cards are super easy to create. All you

do is:

- Find the video you want to add cards to and select "edit video."
- In tab at the top, select "cards."
- Select "add card" and choose the type of card you want. (I prefer "link cards" - but you can choose whichever one you want.)
- Click on "create"
- "Enable" cards - if you haven't done so yet. (You'll have to accept terms and conditions. Don't worry - they won't make you give up your first-born. Yet.)
- Enter the URL where you wanna send people.
- Upload an image. (Be mindful the image will be cropped to a sqaure.)
- Edit your title and call to action in the card. (Keep it simple. Don't get complicated. Tell 'em what they'll get by

clicking.)

- Set a time for when you want the card to appear. (I'd say get one in within the first 30 seconds - and then space 'em out from there.) Don't put in more than three cards per video.
- Click on "create card" and you're done!

Inside YouTube Promo Strategy No. 2: Create Keyword-Friendly Playlists

Here's another technique a lot of YouTube creators miss out on. (And it's so frickin' easy.)

All you do is create a playlist around a specific keyword that includes your videos and a mix of other people's videos.

The key thing here is to include other people's stuff, not just your own. However, avoid adding your competitor's videos, unless you would like to help their business out.

To create your own YouTube playlist just:

- Click on "add to" underneath the video you want to add the playlist
- Choose a keyword-friendly playlist name
- Add some other videos that you didn't create

Bonus points: If you're feeling super-ninja you could head over to Fiverr and purchase some SEO gigs that point backlinks to the playlist URL. (But only if you're feeling super-ninja. If you're feeling just slightly ninja, then I would avoid.)

Inside YouTube Promo Strategy No. 3: Respond to Comments Within 24 Hours

I must admit, I'm not as good about this as I should be. But one of the biggest factors in determining the "authority" of your YouTube channel is your engagement with people who leave comments.

Especially within a day of the comment being left.

So, try to check in every couple of days to respond to comments. (You should get an email each time a comment is left.)

But…PLEASE…do not engage with negative commenters. (It's not worth it. Trust me.)

Inside YouTube Promo Strategy No.4: Build Your Subscriber Base Fast!

The best thing about subscribers is they comment. (Sometimes too much.)

And even more importantly, subscribers get an email from YouTube every time you upload a new video. This ensures all your future videos will have plenty of social buzz around them.

So, what's the catch?

Well, doing this is a manual process. (In the next chapter, I'll show you a tool that can help automate it.)

One of the most effective ways that I've found that boosted the views of my YouTube videos, literally overnight, is to "send messages" to my target audience inviting them to:

Check out my new video and/or subscribe to my channel.

Say I run an e-commerce site that specializes in Minor League Baseball apparel. (An interesting market.)

Well, instead of spending tons of money on Google PPC traffic, I could create a video on the Top 5 Coolest Baseball Caps in Minor League Baseball.

And then I could find out who the fans of those teams are, by searching for videos relating to those teams. (And sending messages to people who've commented on those videos.)

It's quite an easy process, you just:

- Search for videos related to your subject.
- Locate people who've commented recently — within the last two months.

- Click on their name to bring up their profile page.
- Click on the "send message" button. (Located in the drop-down arrow on the right side, under their name.)
- Send them a message like: "Hey. I noticed you're a fan of the Sacramento Bear Cats. I just made a video of the Top 5 Baseball caps in Minor League baseball and they made the cut. Thought you'd want to check it out. Thanks!"

Now, I know that sounds quite manual. (It is.)

I'll show you a tool in the next chapter that can handle it super easily, but in the interim maybe you could get an intern or some aimless teenager (maybe one who shares your last name) to do it for you.

No joke, this one technique will put your face in front hundreds of new people each day, and if you follow it up with the rest of the techniques in this chapter, you'll be dominating the YouTube universe in no time.

Chapter Six Key Takeaways:

- Promote your YouTube video by sharing your unique URL on your various social media properties.
- Buy a few SEO gigs over at Fiverr.com to build some keyword-focused backlinks to your video.
- Write and distribute a press release about your video. (Nobody does this.)
- Create YouTube cards for your videos that have clear calls-to-action AND links to your external site.
- Build keyword-friendly YouTube playlists for extra exposure.
- Try to respond to all comments to your video within a day or two. (Skip the negative ones.)
- Send messages to commenters of similar videos inviting them to subscribe to your channel.

Chapter 7: Super Advanced Ninja YouTube Tactics

"Great thoughts speak to the thoughtful mind, but great actions speak to all mankind."

-Emily P. Bissell

Before we jump into the deep part of the video marketing tool, let me just say…

…if you follow the tips I've outlined so far, and there's not a ton of competition out there for you in the YouTube stratosphere, then everything we've gone over to this point should be enough.

If you're a local business, chances are the

restaurant or business down the street will not be employing the same strategies. And you're likely to crush them on the video side in a matter of weeks.

But if you're in a more-competitive market, say something in the weight-loss or financial-services markets, then you're going to find there are a lot more animals at the trough.

So, below are my THREE Super-Advanced YouTube Marketing Tactics you can use to destroy the competition and reign supreme as the YouTube King of your market:

Warning: These tactics are a bit technical and dorky. Consult your local teenage hacker if the methods detailed aren't clear.

Ninja Promo Tactic No.1: Tube Buddy

I know. I went over this tactic in Chapter 5.

But Tube Buddy is so powerful, and FREE, I'm going to reiterate again.

If you want to know:

- What video topics to cover
- What to title your video
- Which tags to use
- When is the best time

Then Tube Buddy is like the YouTube Obi-Wan Kenobi you deserve. (Hopefully Tube Buddy won't ever cut off a guys' arm in a bar. But you never know.)

Seriously, I use this tool every day and I can't recommend it enough.

Ninja Promo Tactic No. 2: Feed the RSS Monster

I'll be honest, I don't really understand how RSS works.

I mean I know what it is. RSS stands for (Really Simple Syndication) and refers to a technology that helps organize and distribute content around the Internet. (RSS Feed readers such as Feedly use them.)

And I also know it is dying as a mode of consuming media. (You can thank Facebook for that.)

But I don't care about any of that. All I care about is how feeds build super-quick bridges to my content. (Namely, my YouTube videos.)

And it works as a quick-and-dirty promotional tool to create little freeways around the Internet that lead straight to my videos.

Now because each of your YouTube videos are static web locations, not a constantly changing feed, you'll have to do a bit of manual work to make this strategy happen. (But it's really, easy.)

Here's what you do:

1. Grab the URL of your YouTube video.
2. Head over to Feedity. (This site allows you to create a feed from a web URL.)
3. Submit your video URL and create a feed.
4. Copy the feed URL Feedity gives you.
5. Head over to Ping-O-Matic and Pingler. (These are pinging sites that let the world

know your RSS feed exists.)

6. Enter your new feed URL in the fields provided, along with your keyword, and ping the feed. (You only must do this once. Not continually.)

Ninja Promo Tactic No. 3: Pay-Per-Click Advertising (Especially Facebook)

Now I'm not suggesting you spend hundreds of dollars a day on PPC ads trying to drive traffic to your YouTube video. (Unless you really, really want to.)

But if you have experience in the PPC waters, such as Google, then on a strict, modest budget you can actually see a nice ROI for sending traffic to your videos.

As long as you know your numbers and know what a YouTube viewer is worth to ya.

That said: my favorite technique for promoting

videos is to actually "upload" that same video to Facebook - don't just share the YouTube link on your Facebook page, but upload the video - and then promote that video with a couple dollars a day on your Facebook page.

Why do this?

Well, two reasons, it's easy to get .01 and .02 cent views on videos uploaded to Facebook. (In almost any niche.)

And if ya get at least 1000 views in a single day (which should be easy to do with a ten dollar spend) everybody who watches your video that day will be added to a "custom audience."

This will let you serve all those folks with retargeting ads for your other stuff.

Now it's a bit beyond this volume to cover Facebook entirely, but let me just say, taking each of your YouTube videos and uploading them to Facebook - and boosting them with a $20-$30 boost over a couple days can dramatically improve your results.

Not to mention help increase the engagement of your Facebook page.

Ninja Promo Tactic No. 4: Your Very Own YouTube Virtual Assistant

Back in the last chapter I talked about how sending private messages to viewers who are in your ideal target audience was the BEST, FASTEST way to build up your subscriber base…

…and get tons and tons of new people in your good old marketing funnel FAST!

My only lament was that, due to YouTube's rather strict messaging policies, it was a bit time-consuming to manually send out these messages.

Well, there is a tool that can automate it for you.

It's called Tube AssistPro (PunkRockMarketing.com/TubeAssist). And in a nutshell, here's what it does:

1. **You find a video with a bunch of commenters or a channel with a**

bunch of subscribers who you'd like to message. (Your ideal customers.)

2. **You create a message template** of what you'd like to say to these commenters. (Example: "Hey There! Check out my new vid on Facebook Satanism!")
3. **Tube Assist Pro scrapes the video** to find the user profile info for all those commenters.
4. **Tube Assist SLOWLY sends out those messages**, over the course of a few days. (Thereby following YouTube's terms of service - and putting your message in front of hundreds, if not thousands of users over the course of a week.)

I've gotten amazing results from it. (And reached a bunch of people I never would have without it.)

And without question, Tube Assist Pro is my absolute secret weapon that helped me GROW an email list of nearly 10K in a matter of three months with just three videos.

Pretty awesome sauce.

I haven't asked you to buy any fancy tools up to this point, and you don't have to have Tube Assist Pro to have YouTube success, but I unreservedly recommend the tool. (The guys are great, the support is awesome, and the forum is friendly and helpful.)

Chapter Seven Key Takeaways:

- To figure out what to title your videos — and which tags to use — consider adding Tube Buddy to your video marketing toolbox.
- Create an RSS Feed of your video and promote by pinging, for added promotional boost
- Use PPC campaigns - with strict budgets - to extend the reach of your videos. Focus specifically on Facebook. (There's real gold in 'dem hills.)
- The author highly, highly recommends Tube Assist for building your subscriber base up, and exponentially increasing your overall video views.

Epilogue: Conquering the World One Video at a Time

In a previous life I wanted to work in radio. (I guess something about working 60 hours a week and living just above the poverty line appealed to me.)

For a brief time I got to work as an intern for a local sports talk radio station. (You know, the kind where two mentally-imbalanced individuals argue about whether the designated hitter is responsible for the downfall of Western civilization.)

I remember late one night I was messing around in the studio, working on my "reel." (This is a demo that a would-be on-air talent sends around in the hopes of getting a job.)

I was doing my melodramatic intro — "Hey all

you sports fans out there! It's Crazy Mike! And I want to hear from YOU!" — when the grizzled, old station director walked by.

He popped his head in and gave me one of the best lessons I've ever learned.

He said, as radio professionals we "experience" the audience as a large group of people. But an audience does not "experience" radio as a member of an audience.

They experience radio as a one-to-one conversation. (One in which they happen to not have access to a microphone.)

And when you say something like "Hey sports fans!" it destroys the intimate connection an audience has with you. And people don't quite feel as emotional about the things you're talking about, nor are they likely to stick around, while you break away to air some car dealership commercials.

And you end up reaching nobody at all.

This YouTube stuff is addicting.

You'll create a series of videos and in a month

you'll have 2,000 views, 100 comments and tons of new leads and you'll think I need to scale this.

I need to make more videos, and get more subscribers, and get more likes, and hire more video people, and buy some latest YouTube Hack automation tool that can do it all in five minutes or less.

Just remember, video works best when the person on camera is having a conversation with one person.

Trying to solve one person's problems. (Maybe even their own.)

People will email you and write to you to say they felt like you were talking just to "them."

Which you were.

If you can stick with that philosophy and not worry about what you look like on camera, or what aspect ratio your video should be, and do at least a couple videos a month…then there is absolutely nobody who can stop you from reaching all your video marketing goals.

And if have any question about video marketing, or if you want to just let me know what you thought of the book, you can drop me a line at michael@punkrockmarekting.com, I'd love to hear from you.

And if you'd be ever so kind to leave me a REVIEW of the book I would be eternally grateful. And promise to be your bestest friend who watches all of your YouTube videos. (Even the ones with the cats who play piano. Especially those!)

Oh, and just one more thing…

A Special FREE Gift for You!

If you'd like FREE instant access to my seminar "How to Make a Damn Good Living With Social Media (Even If You Hate Social Media" then head over to **PunkRockMarketing.com/Free**. (What else you gonna do? Watch another "Twilight" movie?!)

DISCLAIMER AND/OR LEGAL NOTICES: Every effort has been made to accurately represent this book and it's potential. Results vary with every individual, and your results may or may not be different from those depicted. No promises, guarantees or warranties, whether stated or implied, have been made that you will produce any specific result from this book. Your efforts are individual and unique, and may vary from those shown. Your success depends on your efforts, background and motivation.

The material in this publication is provided for educational and informational purposes only and is not intended as BUSINESS adviceUse of the programs, advice, and information contained in this book is at the sole choice and risk of the reader.

Made in the USA
Monee, IL
08 November 2026

67994715R00069